Horses

by Robin Nelson

first step nonfiction

Lerner Publications Company · Minneapolis

What lives on a farm?

Horses live on a farm.

A female horse is a **mare**.

A male horse is a **stallion**.

Horses have a **mane**.

A horse's foot is called a **hoof**.

Horses have a tail.

They use their tails to shoo
away flies.

Horses eat grass, hay, corn, and oats.

Horses drink a lot of water.

People work with horses.

Horses help move other animals.

Horses help pull things on the farm.

It is fun to see horses on the farm!

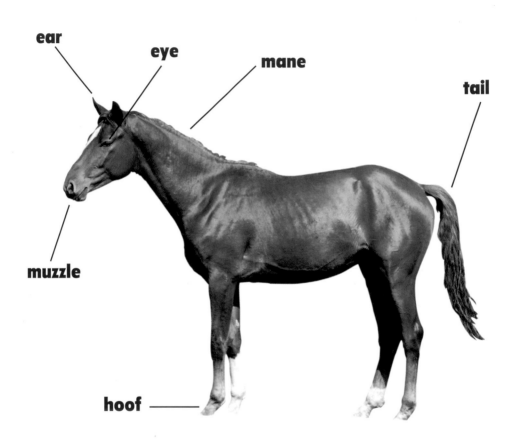

ear

eye

mane

tail

muzzle

hoof

Parts of a Horse

There are many different kinds of horses. Horses can be many different colors—brown, black, gray, and white.

A horse's mouth and nose is called a muzzle. Horses wear metal horseshoes to protect their hooves, or feet.

Horse Facts

 Horses can sleep standing up.

 When you hear a horse neigh, it is talking to another horse.

 A horse greets a friend with a whinny, which is a soft, low neigh.

 There are at least 114 different kinds of horses.

People measure how tall a horse is from the ground to its back. They use a measure called a hand. The biggest horses are about 18 hands, which is 6 feet tall.

A family group of horses is called a band.

A foal can find its mother by her smell.

Glossary

 foal – a baby horse

 hoof – a horse's foot

 mane – hair on the top of a horse's neck

 mare – a female horse

 stallion – a male horse

Index

The images in this book are used with the permission of: © age fotostock/SuperStock, pp. 2, 4; © Lynn M. Stone/naturepl.com, p. 3; © Carol Walker/naturepl.com, pp. 5, 6; © Michael Kelley/The Image Bank/Getty Images, p. 7; © Medford Taylor/National Geographic/Getty Images, p. 8; © Jeanne White/Photo Researchers, Inc., p. 9; © Dick Canby/DRK PHOTO, p. 10; © Andy Ryan/Taxi/Getty Images, p. 11; © David Lyons/Alamy, p. 12; © Philip Nealey/Digital Vision/Getty Images, p. 13; © iStockphoto.com/Rebecca Grabill, p. 14; © William Albert Allard/National Geographic/Getty Images, p. 15; © Jane Therese/drr.net, p. 16; © Michael P. Cardacino/Mira.com/drr.net, p. 17; © Fotolia.com - Otmar Smit, p. 18. Cover: © Rex A. Stucky/National Geographic/Getty Images.

Lerner Publications Company
A division of Lerner Publishing Group, Inc.
241 First Avenue North
Minneapolis, MN 55401 U.S.A.

Website address: www.lernerbooks.com

Library of Congress Cataloging-in-Publication Data

Nelson, Robin, 1971–
    Horses / by Robin Nelson.
        p.   cm. — (First step nonfiction. Farm animals)
    Includes index.
    ISBN 978–0–7613–4058–4 (lib. bdg. : alk. paper)
    1. Horses—Juvenile literature. I. Title.
    SF302.N457 2009
    636.1—dc22   2008024739

Manufactured in the United States of America
2 – DP – 11/1/09